Veg World

Veg World

A Collection of One Hundred Delicious Vegetarian Recipes

DEEPALI PARESH KHONA

PARTRIDGE

To order additional copies of this book, contact
Partridge India
000 800 10062 62
orders.india@partridgepublishing.com

www.partridgepublishing.com/india

CONTENTS

DIPS AND DRINKS

DRINKS

RAITA

SNACKS AND STARTERS

CURRIES

RICE

ROTIS AND BREADS

DESERTS

INTRODUCTION

Dear Reader,

There are lots of good recipe books available but once one gets down to planning a meal, there is invariably some confusion on what goes well with what. This book comes as a simple attempt to give its readers some ideas and practices that help convert a recipe into a perfect meal.

Vegetables are nature's gift to us – low in calories and containing innumerable vitamins, minerals and antioxidants to fight disease.

Nutritionists suggest that we should eat at least 3-5 servings of vegetables daily to fulfill our nutrient requirements. This book teaches us how to make a range of nutritious, low calorie and appetizing recipes.

I have suggested simple menus for entertaining family and friends at different meal times during the day. I hope this book makes your menu planning an easier and more joyful experience.

So get ready to alter your cooking habits so that you can make nutritious and delicious meal for your family and friends.

Warm Regards,
Deepali Paresh Khona

SOUPS AND SALADS

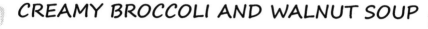

CREAMY BROCCOLI AND WALNUT SOUP

Ingredients :

- 1 Head Broccoli chopped
- 2-3 walnuts
- 1 large onion chopped
- 2 cloves garlic
- 1 large potatoes boiled and cubed
- ½ tsp Black pepper powder
- 1 tsp coconut milk
- ¼ tsp nutmeg powder
- Salt to taste
- ½ cup water

Let's Cook :

In a deep pan over medium heat melt butter. Stir in onion and garlic and cook until onion is translucent.

Stir in Broccoli and boiled potatoes sauté for few seconds. Pour in water and bring to a boil. Cover, reduce heat and simmer until vegetables are tender. Remove from heat.

Once the vegetables are cooked well transfer it into a blender, puree it by adding salt, pepper, nutmeg. Again bring to boil for few minutes and serve hot garnished with coconut milk and chopped walnuts.

POTATO AND SPINACH SOUP

Ingredients :
- Potatoes boiled & peeled – 2 medium
- Spinach blanched – 1 medium bunch
- Oil – 2 tbsp
- Onions – 2 medium
- Garlic – 3 – 4 cloves
- Milk – ½ cup
- Black pepper powder – 1
- Vegetable stock or water
- Salt to taste

Let's Cook :

Heat oil in a deep non-stick pan. Chop onions roughly and add along with garlic and saute, roughly chopped spinach and crush potatoes add to the pan.

Add 2 cups water or stock and salt and cook till onions are soft, strain and let it cool. Then grind till smooth.

Put the strained stock back in the pan, add milk, pepper powder, salt and let it come to a boil. Pour in a soup bowl and serve hot.

TOMATO BASIL SOUP

Ingredients :
- Tomatoes roughly chopped – 5-6
- Onions – 2 medium
- Olive oil – 2 tbsp
- Garlic – 3-4 cloves
- Salt to taste
- Black pepper powder – ½ tsp
- Fresh basil leaves – 3-4
- Bread slices - 4

Let's Cook :

Heat oil in a pressure cooker. Roughly chop onions. Add cumin seeds, onions and sauté. Crush garlic and add along with tomatoes. Mix and add salt, black pepper and 3 cups water.

Close the cooker and cook under pressure till 2-3 whistles are given out. Open the lid when the pressure reduces and transfer the mixture into a blender jar and let it cool.

Trim the edges of bread slices and add to the blender jar. Add basil leaves and blend everything till smooth.

Pour the soup back into the pan and heat serve hot garnishing with basil leaves.

CLEAR VEGETABLE SOUP

Ingredients:

- Cabbage – ¼
- Onion – 1 medium
- Celery – 2 inches
- Salt to taste
- Corn kernels – ¼ cup
- Brocoli – 4-5 florets
- Carrots – 1 medium
- Black pepper powder to taste
- Vegetable stock

Let's Cook :

In a non-stick pan heat oil, add onions, cabbage, corn, carrots broccoli and sauté. Add vegetable stock and let it come to boil. Add salt, black pepper powder, celery and again allow it to boil. Pour into soup bowl and serve hot.

VEGETABLE MANCHOW SOUP

Ingredients :

- Carrots chopped – 1 medium
- Cabbage chopped – ¼ small
- Green capsicum chopped – ½ medium
- Spring onion – 1
- Oil – 2 tbsp
- Ginger – ½ inch piece
- Garlic chopped – 2-3 cloves
- Green chillies – 2
- Red chilli sauce – ½ tbsp
- Soy sauce – 2 tbsp
- Tofu – 50 g
- Cornflour – 3 tbsp
- Salt to taste
- Noodle deep fried – 1 Cup
- Vegetable stock – 4 Cups

Let's Cook :

Heat oil in a pan, add sliced spring onions, ginger and garlic and toss. Add carrots, cabbage, green chillies to the pan. Add 4 cups stock. Then add red chilli sauce, soy sauce and mix. Cut tofu into ½ inch cubes and add to the soup. Mix cornflour with ¼ cup water and add to the soup and cook till it thickens. Add salt and mix chop capsicum, reserve some for garnish and add rest to the soup and mix well. Serve the soup hot garnished with fried noodles and capsicum.

SWEET CORN VEGETABLE SOUP

Ingredients :

- Sweet corn kernals boiled – ½ cup
- Sweet corn cream style – 2 cups
- Oil – 1 tbsp
- Cabbage grated – ¼ cup
- Carrots finely chopped – ¼ medium
- Vegetables stock – 4 cups
- White pepper powder – ½ tsp
- Salt to taste
- Cornflour – 3 tbsp

Let's Cook :

Heat oil in a non-stick wok. Grate cabbage and add to the hot oil. Add carrot and sauté on high heat for 1-2 minutes.

Add cream style corn and mix well. Add 4 cups veg stock and mix and allow it to come to a boil.

Mix pepper powder in 2 tbsp water and add to the soup along with salt and mix well.

Add corn kernels and allow it to come to a boil again. Mix cornflour in 2 tbsp water and add to the soup and cook till it thickens, serve hot.

CABBAGE, PEAS AND ALMOND SOUP

Ingredients :

- Butter – 1 tbsp
- Cabbage – bowl
- Green peas – ¼ cup
- Almond paste – 1 tbsp
- Cheese spread – 1 tbsp
- Salt to taste
- Sugar – 1 tbsp
- Black pepper powder – 1 tbsp

Let's Cook :

Heat butter in a pressure cooker. Add cabbage and green peas and sauté. Then add water and close the lid and cook under pressure till 2-3 whistles are given out. Allow it to cool.

Take another pan and heat. Put the mixture in a blender jar and grind to a smooth paste. Pour the paste in a hot pan, add water, salt, black pepper, sugar and allow it to come to boil. Then add almond paste and cheese spread. Cook till it thickens, pour the soup in a soup bowl and garnish it with almond slices and serve hot.

GREEN PEAS AND MINT SOUP

Ingredients :

- 2 cups fresh green peas.
- 1 tsp butter
- ¼ cup chopped onions
- ½ cup milk
- ½ tsp black pepper powder
- 1 tbsp finely chopped mint leaves
- Salt to taste

Let's Cook :

Heat the butter in a non stick pan, add onions and sauté on a medium for a few minutes.

Add green peas, 1 ½ cups of water and salt and bring to boil.

Simmer for 15 mns or till the peas are cooked. Cool and blend in a mixer to a smooth puree and keep aside.

Combine ½ cup water and ½ cup milk in a deep pan, add green peas puree, mix well and cook on a medium flame for 3-4 mins.

Add pepper, mint leaves, salt to taste and cook on medium flame for 1-2 mins.

Serve hot garnished with mint leaves.

CAPSICUM AND BEAN SPROUTS STIR FRY SOUP

Ingredients :

- 1 cup finely sliced Red capsicum. (Red Bell pepper)
- ½ cup Bean sprouts
- 1 tbsp oil
- ½ cup thinly sliced onions
- Salt to taste
- Black pepper powder to taste
- 1 tbsp chopped coriander leaves.

Let's Cook :

Heat the oil in a pan, add onions and sauté an a high flame for 2-3 mnts.

Add the red capsicum and bean sprouts and sauté on a high flame for 2-3 minutes.

Add 3 cups of hot water and salt and mix well. Cook on a high flame for 2-3 minutes.

Switch off the flame, add the pepper powder and mix well.

Serve hot garnished with coriander leaves.

GREEN PEAS AND CORN SOUP

Ingredients :

- 2 cups green peas
- ¼ cup chopped onions
- 1 clove of garlic
- Salt to taste
- ¼ tsp chilli powder
- 1 cup boiled sweet corn kernels
- Black pepper powder 1 tbsp
- 1 tbsp all purpose flour (maida)
- 1 tbsp butter

Let's Cook :

Heat butter in a pan, add onions garlic and saute. Add green peas, maida and sauté. Add 1 cup water and pressure cook for 2-3 whistles.

Allow the steam to escape before opening and then blend in a mixer to a smooth puree.

Pour in a non-stick pan, add chilli powder, sweet corn kernels, salt, pepper and ½ cup of water and bring to boil. Serve hot.

SALADS

RUSSIAN SALAD

Ingredients :

- Mix vegetables boiled 1 bowl.
  (potato, carrots, beans, green peas)
- Onions finely chopped 1 small
- Mayonnaise – 2 tbsp
- Fresh cream – 2 tbsp
- Curd – 2 tbsp
- Salt to taste
- Black pepper powder – 1 tbsp
- Coriander leaves – 1-2 tbsp

Let's Cook :

Boil mix vegetables and cut into cubes. In a bowl add vegetables, chopped onions, mayonnaise, fresh cream, curd and mix well. Add salt, pepper powder and again mix them well. Serve the salad garnished with coriander leaves.

CABBAGE BENGAL GRAM SALAD

Ingredients :
- Mix Vegetables – 1 bowl
  (Cabbage, Carrots, tomatoes, cucumbers)
- Soaked and boiled Bengal gram – 2 tbsp

Dressing :
- Ginger juice – 1 tsp
- Vinegar – 1 tbsp
- Salt – 1 tsp
- Olive oil – 1 tbsp
- Lemon juice – 1 tsp
- Black pepper powder – ½ tbsp
- Sugar – 1 tsp
- Mint leaves chopped – 1 tbsp
- Coriander leaves – 1 tbsp

Let's Cook :
Boil the soaked Bengal gram, chop cabbage, carrots, cucumber and tomatoes finely in a bowl. Mix vegetables and Bengal gram. Pour dressing and mix well serve salad garnish with mint leaves and coriander leaves.

BROKEN WHEAT SALAD

Ingredients :
- Boiled broken wheat – 1 cup
- Finely chopped tomatoes – 1 medium
- Finely chopped capsicum – 1 small
- Roasted almonds – 3-4
- Cashew nuts – 8 – 10
- Apricots – 2-3
- Salt to taste
- Black pepper powder – 1 tbsp
- Lime juice – 1 tbsp
- Finely chopped Onions – 1 small
- Coriander leaves

Let's Cook :

Boil broken wheat in a pressure cooker. Allow it to cool. In a bowl take broken wheat, add onions, tomatoes, capsicum, roasted almonds, cashewnuts and apricots and mix well. Add salt, pepper powder, lime juice and mix well. Serve the salad garnished with chopped coriander leaves.

SWEET CORN SALAD

Ingredients :
- Boiled sweet corn kernels – 1 cup
- Fresh basil leaves 3-4
- Red & Green peppers chopped – ¼ cup

Dressing :
- Mayonnaise – 1 tbsp
- Salt to taste
- Black pepper powder – 1 tbsp
- Vinegar – 1 tbsp

Let's Cook :

In a small bowl prepare dressing by mixing all the ingredients and keep aside.

Take another bowl add boiled sweet corn and red and green peppers. Add dressing and mix well. Add finely chopped basil leaves. Serve the salad garnished with basil leaves.

AVOCADO SALAD

Ingredients :
- 3-4 fresh large tomatoes sliced.
- ½ onion sliced
- 2 avocados peeled and cut into small cubes
- ¼ cup chopped fresh parsley
- 1 garlic clove, minced
- 2 tbsp dried oregano
- 1 tbsp vinegar
- 1 tbsp olive oil
- Black pepper powder – 1 tbsp
- Salt to taste

Let's Cook :

Place a layer of sliced tomatoes on a large serving platter. Arrange the onion slices and avocados over the tomatoes sprinkle parsley, garlic and oregano. Drizzle vinegar and olive oil over the platter. Sprinkle with salt and freshly ground black pepper. Serve immediately. Do not refrigerate.

ROASTED CORN CORB AND CORNFLAKES SALAD

Ingredients :
- Corn corb – 1
- Cornflakes crushed – ½ cup
- Butter – 1 tbsp
- Oil – 1 tbsp
- Garlic cloves minced – 6-8
- Finely chopped green chillies – 1
- Honey – 1 tbsp
- Juice of 1 lemon
- Red chilli flakes – ¼ tsp
- Crushed black pepper corns – ¼ tsp
- Salt to taste
- Chat masala – ¼ tsp
- Onion cut into cubes – 1 medium
- Tomato cubed – 1 medium
- Red chilli powder – ¼ tsp
- Coriander leaves – 2 tsp

Let's Cook :

Roast the corn corb on direct heat till well done. Heat butter and oil in a non-stick pan, add garlic and sauté on a low heat. Transfer into a bowl.

Add green chilli, honey, lemon juice, red chilli flakes, black pepper corns, salt, chat masala, onions and tomato and mix well. Separate the roasted corns from the corb and add to the bowl and mix. Add 1 tsp coriander leaves and mix. Garnish with remaining coriander leaves, chat masala, red chilli powder and crushed cornflakes and serve immediately.

GUAVA AND SPROUTS SALAD

Ingredients :
- 1 cup finely chopped green guavas
- 1 cup green gram sprouts (moong sprouts)
- ½ cup fresh sweet corn
- ¼ cup finely chopped red onion
- 1 tbsp lime juice
- Coriander leaves – 2 tbsp
- Black pepper powder – 1 tbsp
- Salt to taste

Let's Cook :

It really can't get simpler than this ! just combine all the ingredients and serve immediately. Make sure all the ingredients are fresh for the best results.

PASTA SALAD

Ingredients :

- ½ cup boiled pasta
- ¼ cup blanched broccoli florets
- ¼ cup chopped pineapple.
- ¼ cup chopped black grapes
- 2 tbsp finely shredded cabbage
- 2 tbsp boiled corn kernels
- 2 tbsp thickly grated carrots
- 2 tbsp chopped almonds

Dressing :

- 2 tbsp pineapple puree
- Salt to taste
- Black pepper powder – 1 tbsp

Let's Cook :

Combine all the ingredients in a bowl and mix well. Refrigerate to chill.

Just before serving pour the dressing and toss well.

Serve immediately.

BEAN CAPSICUM SALAD

Ingredients :

- 1 ½ cups soaked and boiled kidney beans
- 1 ½ cups soaked and boiled chickpeas
- 1 Red capsicum
- ½ tsp oil for brushing
- ½ cup finely chopped onions
- ¼ cup finely chopped coriander
- 1 ½ tsp lemon juice
- ½ tsp chilli powder
- 2 tsp finely chopped green chillies
- Salt to taste

Let's Cook :

Pierce a fork through the capsicum brush oil evenly over it and roast on a slow flame till it turns black in colour from all the sides.

Immerse the capsicum in cold water, remove the skin, stem and seeds and thinly slice it.

Combine all the ingredients including the capsicum in a deep bowl and toss well.

Serve chilled.

THAI GREEN PAPAYA SALAD

Ingredients :

For the Sauce :   4 tbsp fresh lime juice

4 tbsp Soy sauce

1.5 tbsp brown sugar

For the Salad

- 4 cloves of garlic
- 5 tbsp unsalted peanuts
- 3-4 red chillies
- 3 tomatoes cut into wedges
- 4 long beans or asparagus cut into 2 inch segments
- 1 cup raw papaya peeled and shredded
- 1 carrot peeled and shredded

Let's Cook :

Combine all the ingredients for sauce and mix until sugar dissolves.

In an another bowl add papaya, carrots, garlic, peanuts, red chillies, tomatoes, beans and pour sauce over it and toss very well. Taste and adjust the flavors with additional lime juice or sugar if necessary.

CHINESE VEG SALAD

Ingredients :
- Finely chopped cucumber – 1 medium
- Finely chopped carrots – 1 medium
- Chopped Red and green bell peppers – ¼ cup
- Finely shredded cabbage – ¼ cup
- Salt to taste
- Soy sauce – 4 tbsp
- Vinegar – 4 tbsp
- Sugar – 3 tbsp
- Sesame oil – 4 tsp
- Red chilli sauce – 1-2 tsp
- Black sesame seeds – 1-2 tbsp

Let's Cook :

In a bowl take all the vegetables and toss it. Add salt, vinegar, soy sauce, red chilli sauce, sugar, sesame oil and mix well.

Serve the salad garnished with black sesame seeds.

DIPS AND DRINKS

CHEESE DIP

Ingredients :
- ½ cup milk
- 4 cheese slices
- 2 tbsp finely chopped bell pepper
- 2 tsp cornflour
- ¼ tsp mustard paste
- Salt to taste

Let's Cook :

In a microwave safe bowl add the milk, cheese slices, bell peppers, cornflour and mix well. Microwave on high power for 2 minutes stirring once after one minute. Remove and allow it to cool.

Add mustard paste, salt and mix well serve dip in a bowl garnished with mustard paste.

AVOCADO DIP

Ingredients :
- 2 ripe avocados
- 2 tbsp finely chopped tomatoes
- 1 ½ tbsp lemon juice
- 2 tbsp finely chopped spring onion whites
- 1 tsp green chillies
- Salt to taste

For serving :
- Baked tortilla chips, potato wedges

Let's Cook :

Cut the avocados into half and scoop out all the pulp. Mash it with the back of a spoon.

Add all the remaining ingredients and mix well. Keep refrigerate for at least an hour. Serve chilled.

Serve with baked tortilla chips and potato wedges.

HUNG CURD DIP

Ingredients :
- Hung curd – 1 cup
- Green chilli – 1
- Garlic – 2 cloves
- Sugar – 1 tsp
- Coriander leaves – ¾ cup
- Salad oil or groundnut oil – 2 tbsp
- Salt to taste

Let's Cook :

Blend all the ingredients with a blender till smooth and creamy. Keep refrigerated.

This dip can be served with stir fried cashews, chips, potato wedges, fresh cucumber and carrots fingers and pakoras.

SPINACH DIP

Ingredients :
- Spinach – 1 medium bunch
- Yogurt – 4 tbsp
- Oil – 1 tbsp
- Onion – 1 medium
- Cottage cheese – 50 gms
- Cream cheese – 50 gms
- Lime juice – 2 tsp
- Salt to taste

Let's Cook :
Heat oil in a non-stick pan. Roughly chop onion and spinach and add salt and saute till all the moisture evaporates.

Transfer into a mixer jar. Roughly chop cottage cheese and add.

Add cream cheese, yogurt, lemon juice and grind to a slightly coarse dip.

Transfer into a bowl and serve at room temperature or chilled.

CHEESE AND CARROT DIP

Ingredients :
- Grated processed cheese – 2 tbsp
- Grated carrot – ½ cup
- Hung curd – 1 ½ cup
- Finely chopped bell peppers – 2 tbsp
- Finely chopped onions – 2 tsp
- Milk – 2 tbsp
- Finely chopped green chillies – 1 tsp
- Fresh cream – 2 tbsp
- Salt to taste

Let's Cook :
Combine all the ingredients in a deep bowl and mix well. Refrigerate for 1 hour and serve chilled.

EASY ASIAN DIPPING SAUCE

Ingredients :
- ½ cup soy sauce
- ½ cup rice wine vinegar
- 2 tbsp honey
- 2 cloves minced garlic
- 2 tbsp minced fresh ginger root
- 2 tsps sesame seeds
- 2 tsps sesame oil

Let's Cook :

Whisk together the soy sauce, vinegar, honey, garlic, ginger, sesame seeds, sesame oil in a bowl. This easy dipping sauce goes well with spring rolls.

WATERMELON AND ICE SALSA

Ingredients :

- 3 cups chopped watermelon
- ½ cup chopped green bell pepper
- 2 tbsp lime juice
- 2 tbsp chopped fresh cilantro
- 1 tbsp chopped green onions
- 1 tbsp chopped jalapeno pepper
- ½ tsp garlic salt

Let's Cook :

In a large bowl, combine the watermelon, green bell pepper, lime juice, cilantro, green onions, jalapeno, garlic and salt mix well and serve it with tortilla chips.

PINEAPPLE SALSA

Ingredients :
- 1 cup diced pineapple
- 1 diced tomato
- 1 sweet onion
- 1 tbsp olive oil
- 1 tsp salt
- 1 tsp garlic powder
- 1 tsp pepper
- 1 red bell pepper diced

Let's Cook :

Combine all ingredients in a large bowl and mix together. Refrigerate for 2 hours before serving. Serve with any type of tortilla chips.

CHUNKY BROCCOLI AND CORN DIP

Ingredients :
- ¼ cup Broccoli florets
- ¼ cup sweet corn kernels
- ½ cup milk
- 2 tsp chopped onions
- Red chilli flakes a pinch
- 1 tbsp maida (All purpose flour)
- 2 tsp butter
- Salt to taste

Let's Cook :

In a microwave safe bowl add broccoli florets and corn kernels along with 1 tbsp of water and microwave on high for 45 seconds.

In another bowl add butter, onions, chilli flakes and microwave for 1 min.

Add the flour, mix well and microwave for 30 sec. Add milk, broccoli, corn kernels, salt and again microwave for 2 minutes.

Your dip is ready to serve. You can serve with bread sticks or with chips or you can toss with pasta to make a salad.

DRINKS

CARROT PINEAPPLE COCKTAIL

Ingredients :
- Pineapple juice – 2 cups
- Carrots – 2 medium
- 1 slice of lemon, ¼ inch thick
- 1 cup crushed ice

Let's Cook :

Put pineapple juice, carrots, lemon into a blender jar and process till carrot is liquified. Remove feeder cap and add ice cubes, continue processing until ice is liquified. Serve chilled garnished with pineapple slice.

COFFEE BANANA COOLER

Ingredients :
- 300 ml milk
- 4 tbsp instant coffee powder
- 150 g vanilla ice cream
- 2 bananas sliced and frozen

Let's Cook :

Pour the milk into a food processor or blender, add the coffee powder and process gently until combined. Add half of the vanilla ice cream and process gently, then add the remaining ice cream and process until well combined.

When the mixture is thoroughly blended, add the bananas and process until smooth.

Pour the mixture into glasses and serve.

CUCUMBER LASSI

Ingredients :

- Cucumber peeled and cubed – 2
- Yogurt – 2 cup
- Ginger – 2 inches
- Coriander leaves – 2 tbsp
- Salt to taste
- Mint leaves – 2 tbsp
- Cumin powder – 1 tbsp
- Ice cubes – 1 cup

Let's Cook :

Blend together all the ingredients. Add ice cubes and blend again. Pour into glasses, chill and serve.

KIWI COOLER

Ingredients :

- 2 cups crushed ice
- 4 tsp sugar syrup
- 8 tbsp kiwi crush
- 4 tbsp lemon juice
- 300 ml chilled soda

Let's Cook :

In a tall glass, place ½ cup of crushed ice.

Pour 1 tsp of sugar syrup, 2 tbsp kiwi crush, 1 tbsp lemon juice over it and stir using a stirrer.

Repeat the step to make 3 more glasses.

Top each glass with chilled soda water and serve immediately garnished with a slice of kiwi.

STRAWBERRY MARGARITA

Ingredients :
- Strawberry crush – ½ cup
- Crushed ice – 3 ½ cups
- Lemon juice – 4 tbsp
- Sugar – 4 tbsp

For the rim
- 1 tbsp lemon juice
- 1 tbsp salt

Let's Cook :

For the rim dip the rim of a glass in lemon juice and then place the glass gently over a glass plate containing salt. Dust of excess salt and keep aside. Repeat the same to make one more glass.

For the drink combine ice, lemon juice, strawberry crush and sugar and blend till smooth. Pour equal quantities of the juice in each salt rimmed glass and serve immediately.

OREO CHOCLATE MILKSHAKE

Ingredients :
- 8 oreo biscuits
- 4 tbsp chocolate syrup
- 1-2 cups of milk
- 2 cups softened vanilla ice-cream or chocolate ice-cream

Let's Cook :

Chop 4 oreo cookies extremely finely and set them aside. The remaining 4 you can cut into large chunks.

Coat four glasses with chocolate syrup, all the way around and add generous amount at the bottom.

Now in the blender you have to add milk, large chunks of oreo cookies and the softened vanilla ice-cream. Blend it for 3-4 min. till you can gain a smooth texture.

Pour it over the chocolate syrup coated glasses.

Top it off with those finely chopped oreo cookies as garnish and serve immediately.

ORANGE PINEAPPLE PUNCH

Ingredients :
- Pineapple juice – 1 cup
- Orange juice – 1 cup
- Lemon juice – 1 tbsp
- Rose syrup – 2 tbsp
- Crushed ice
- Soda as required

Let's Cook :

In a mixer pour pineapple juice, orange juice, lemon juice and ice. Add rose syrup and blend well. Pour into a glass till three fourth and remaining one-fourth fill with soda or as required. Garnish with orange pieces and serve chilled.

BLACK GRAPE COOLER

Ingredients :

- Black grape juice – 4 cups
- Cumin seeds – 3/4 tbsp
- Saunf – 1 tsp (Fennel seeds)
- Carom seeds – ½ tsp
- Black salt – 3 tsp
- Crushed ice – 1 cup
- Mint leaves
- Tamarind pulp – 1 ½ tbsp

Let's Cook :

Dry roast the cumin seeds, fennel seeds, carom seeds and grind with black salt to a fine powder. Place the ice and tamarind pulp in a blender.

Pour the grape juice and add the powdered spices. Blend all the ingredients together.

Place the mint leaves in individual glasses. Pour the grape cooler in the glasses and serve chilled.

PEACH TANGO

Ingredients :
- 3 peaches cut into halves
- 1 tsp ginger juice
- 1 ½ tsp lemon juice
- 3 tbsp sugar syrup
- 1 cup crushed ice

For garnishing :
- 8 ginger juliennes
- 4 parsley leaves

Let's Cook :

Freeze the peaches in the freezer till they are hard. Combine the peaches, ginger juice, lemon juice, sugar syrup and ice into a mixer and blend till slushy.

In each glass pour equal quantity of drink and garnish with 2 ginger juliennes and a parsley leaf. Serve immediately.

FOREST FRUIT SMOOTHIE

Ingredients :
- 350 ml orange juice
- 1 banana slice and frozen
- 450 g frozen forest fruits

(Such as blue berries, raspberries and black berries)
- Slice of orange to garnish

Let's Cook :

Pour the orange juice into a food processor or blender. Add the banana and half of the forest fruits and process until smooth.

Add the remaining forest fruits and process until smooth.

Pour the mixture into glasses and decorate the rims with slices of orange.

FIG AND MAPLE MELTER

Ingredients :
- 350 ml hazelnut yogurt
- 2 tbsp freshly squeezed orange juice
- 4 tbsp maple syrup
- 8 large fresh figs chopped
- Ice cubes
- Toasted chopped hazelnuts for garnishing

Let's Cook :

Pour the yogurt, orange juice and maple syrup into a blender and process gently until combined.

Add the figs and ice cubes and process until smooth.

Pour the mixture into glasses and scatter over some toasted chopped hazelnuts.

Serve chilled.

RAITA

PINEAPPLE RAITA

Ingredients :
- ½ cup chopped canned pineapple.
- 1 cup thick beaten curd
- 2 tsp grated ginger
- 1 tsp finely chopped green chillies
- 1 tsp powdered sugar
- 1 tsp black pepper powder.
- Salt to taste
- 2 tsp chopped coriander leaves
- A pinch roasted cumin powder.

Let's Cook :

Combine all the ingredients in a bowl and mix well. Serve chilled.

SPINACH RAITA

Ingredients :

- 2 cups chopped spinach
- 1 tsp oil
- ½ tsp cumin seeds
- Pinch of asafoetida
- 2 whole red chillies
- ½ tsp black pepper powder
- ½ tsp salt
- 1 ½ cup yogurt

Let's Cook :

Heat the oil in a sauce pan on medium high heat. Add cumin seeds, asafoetida. After the cumin seeds crackle add whole red chillies and stir fry for few seconds.

Add spinach, salt and black pepper and stir fry pressing the spinach down to allow most of the water to evaporate but still leaving the spinach moist.

After the spinach cools off, mix it well into yogurt. Add milk to the raita about half a cup to adjust the desired consistency. Serve chilled.

AVOCADO AND POMEGRANATE RAITA

Ingredients :

- 1 ripe Avocado peeled
- 1 ½ cup plain yogurt
- ½ - ¾ cup pomegranate seeds
- 1 green chilli chopped
- Coriander leaves chopped
- Salt to taste
- ½ tsp sugar
- 1 tsp roasted cumin powder
- 1 – 1 ½ tsp lemon juice
- ½ tsp chat masala
-

Let's Cook :

Take peeled Avocado and chop it up into small bits. Put avocado bits into blender. Add 2-3 tbsp yogurt, salt, sugar, coriander, green chilli and blend them together to form a smooth paste.

In another bowl, pour yogurt and beat it gently. Add avocado mixture. Finally add pomegranate seeds and coriander leaves. Chill the raita before serving.

MIX FRUIT RAITA

Ingredients :
- ¼ cup chopped apple
- ¼ cup chopped canned pineapple
- ¼ cup kiwi chopped.
- ¼ cup pomegranate seeds.
- ¼ cup strawberry's chopped
- ¼ cup orange peeled
- 2 cups Beaten curd
- ¼ cup chopped mint leaves
- ¼ cup low fat milk
- 1 tsp black pepper
- Salt to taste
- Chopped coriander leaves
- Sugar to taste

Let's Cook :
In a bowl take beaten curd, add salt, sugar, black salt, black pepper, mint leaves and coriander leaves and mix well.

Add chopped fruits to the mixture and serve chilled.

MIX VEG RAITA

Ingredients :

- 3 Cups beaten curd
- 1 carrot grated
- 1 cucumber finely chopped
- 1 tomato finely chopped
- 1 onion finely chopped
- 2-3 tbsp coriander leaves
- A pinch of black salt
- Salt to taste
- 2 tsp cumin seeds powder.
- 1 tsp red chilli powder
- 1 green chilli finely chopped.

Let's Cook :

Beat the curd till smooth. Add all the ingredients chill and serve garnished with fresh coriander and a pinch of red chilli powder.

SWEET CORN AND BOONDI RAITA

Ingredients :

- Sweet corn boiled – 1 cup
- Boondi – ½ cup
- Yogurt – 2 cups
- Coriander leaves – ¼ cup
- Mint leaves – ¼ cup
- Green chilli – 1
- Salt to taste
- Cumin powder ½ tsp
- Sugar – 2 tbsp
- Black salt – ¼ tsp
- Red chilli powder – 1 pinch

Let's Cook :

Grind coriander leaves, mint leaves, green chilli and 2 tbsp curd to a fine paste. Mix this with remaining yogurt well.

Add salt, cumin, black salt, sugar and mix well. Drain sweet corn and add to the yogurt and mix well. Add boondi, mix and serve chilled garnished with little boondi and sprinkled with a red chilli powder.

SNACKS AND STARTERS

GREEN GRAM (MOONG DAL) KACHORI

Ingredients :

- Skinless green gram – ½ cup
- Wheat flour – 1 ½ cups
- Salt to taste
- Oil – 6 tbsp
- Asafoetida a pinch
- Ginger finely chopped – 1 inch pc.
- Green chillies chopped – 2
- Garam masala – 1 tsp
- Red chilli powder – 2 tsp
- Amchur (green mango) powder – 1 tsp

Let's Cook :

Take whole wheat flour in a bowl. Add salt, 4 tbsp oil and mix. Add sufficient water and knead into a medium soft dough.

Boil the moong dal in a half cup of water till just cooked and dry. Add 2 tbsp oil in a pan, add asafoetida, ginger, green chillies, moong dal, garam masala, red chilli powder, amchur, salt and mix. Sauté for few minutes.

Remove from heat and transfer into a bowl and mash lightly. Divide the dough into even sized balls.

Roll them slightly, put the stuffing's and gather the edges to seal.

Roll into a ball again and flatten slightly. Roll as for puries with hand or rolling pin. Heat sufficient oil in a wok and fry the kachories till light golden. Serve hot with green coriander chutney or tomato ketchup.

ZUCCHINI CUPS STUFFED WITH ROASTED BELL PEPPER

Ingredients :
- 2 Zucchini
- 1/3 cup chopped roasted red bell pepper
- 1/3 cup crumbled feta cheese
- 2 tbsp toasted pine nuts chopped
- ½ tsp dried oregano
- Pepper to taste

Let's Cook :

To make zucchini cups, trim and discard the zucchini ends. Cut the zucchini diagonally into 3/4th inch thick slices. Using a melon scooper, take out the centre of each slice, leaving a shell to fill the stuffing. Steam the cups in a covered steamer over boiling water for about 4 minutes. Arrange the cups in a dish in a single layer, scooped side up.

Cover lightly and microwave for about 2 minutes. Drain the cups upside down on a plate lined with a paper towel.

To make the stuffing, mix together the chopped bell pepper, feta cheese, pine nuts, oregano and pepper.

Before serving, fill the stuffing in each of the zucchini cups.

Place in a preheated oven for about 3 minutes or until the cheese is softened and lightly browned. Serve warm.

NACHOS SUPREME

Ingredients :
- 1 large pckt nacho chips
- 1 small bottle tomato salsa
- 400 gms cheddar cheese grated
- 200 gms jalapenos chopped
- ¾ cup sour cream.

For the guacamole :
- 2 large ripe avocados
- 1 onion finely chopped
- 1 tomato finely chopped
- 1 lime juice
- Salt and pepper to taste

Let's Cook :

To make the guacamole, remove the flesh from the avocado mash it with a fork.

Add the chopped onions, tomatoes, lime juice, salt and pepper, mix well and keep aside.

To serve take a large oven proof serving dish and spread the nacho chips. Pour the tomato salsa, jalapenos and grated cheddar cheese.

Grill in the oven till the cheese melts. Spread the guacamole and sour cream and serve immediately.

STIR FRIED WATER CHESTNUTS AND LONG BEANS

Ingredients :

- 1 tsp garlic, chopped finely
- 3 dried red chillies coarsely sliced
- ½ cup roasted cashew nuts
- 1 small bundle long beans, chopped into 1 inch length
- 1 cup whole peeled water chestnuts
- 3 tbsp vegetable stock
- 1 tbsp dark soy sauce
- 1 tbsp light soy sauce
- ½ tsp sugar
- 2 tbsp olive oil
- 1 tsp red chilli sauce

Let's Cook :

Heat the oil in a pan and fry the garlic until golden brown.

Add the chopped red chillies, chopped long beans, water chestnuts and mix well.

Pour in the vegetables stock and both the soy sauce, red chilli sauce along with sugar, mix well until the vegetables are coated well with the sauce. Cook for a few mins. Sprinkle the cashew nuts and turn on to a serving dish garnished with coriander leaves.

STIR FRIED VEGETARIAN GLASS NOODLES (MALAYSIAN STYLE)

Ingredients :

- 2 ounces dried glass noodles.
- 2 tbsp tamarind paste
- 2 tsp soy sauce
- 1 tsp Indonesian sweet soy sauce
- 1 tsp sesame oil
- ½ tsp hot chilli paste
- 2 tbsp thai chilli sauce
- 1 tbsp fresh lime juice
- ½ fresh thai chilli pepper speeded and minced.
- 3 tbsp canola or other vegetable oil
- 2 cloves garlic minced
- ½ cup julienned carrots
- ½ cup Chinese garlic chives
- ½ cup trimmed julienned green beans
- 1 cup bean sprouts
- ½ lime cut into wedges

Let's Cook :

For the noodles soak the dried glass noodles in 4 cups of warm water for 30 minutes. Drain and set aside. While the noodles are soaking, prepare the cooking sauce and the garnish sauce.

For the cooking sauce :

In a small bowl mix the tamarind paste with soy sauce, Indonesian sweet soy sauce, sesame oil and hot chilli paste. Mix well and set aside.

To finish and serve :

Place a wok or large sauté pan over medium high heat. Add 3 tbsp of the canola oil and heat until shimmering. Add garlic and cook until fragrant but not brown, about 30 seconds. Add carrots, garlic chives and green beans and stir fry until crisp – tender, 1-2 minutes. Add noodles and continue to stir vigorously to keep the noodles from sticking about 2 minutes. Add the cooking sauce and bean sprouts; toss well and stir fry for 1-2 minutes. Drizzle the garnish sauce on the top of the noodles as desired, and serve with lime wedges on the side.

CRISP CINNAMON FINGERS

Ingredients :

- White or brown bread 4 slices
- Fresh ground cinnamon – 2 tsp
- Sugar – 5 tsp
- Butter – 4 tsp

Let's Cook :

Grind cinnamon and sugar together. Mix it well with butter and spread it evenly on the bread.

Toast it lightly in an oven to melt the sugar. Cut into fingers and drizzle powdered sugar on it before serving.

GRILLED COTTAGE CHEESE (PANEER) ROLLS

Ingredients :
- For the dough
- 1 cup all purpose flour
- 2-3 tbsp curd
- Salt to taste

For the stuffing :
- 1 cup paneer grated
- 5-6 cups spinach boiled and chopped
- 1 cup finely chopped bell pepper
- 1-2 green chillies finely chopped
- 1 tsp chat masala
- Salt to taste

For the sauce :
- 1-2 garlic cloves
- 2 green onions copped
- 3 tbsp tomato ketchup

Let's Cook :

To make the dough, mix all the ingredients into a soft dough make some small rotis and cook on a griddle but not very well done. Keep it aside.

Mix all the ingredients for the filling and make long cutlets. Shallow fry or deep fry it. Put it in the centre of the roti and roll it up like a roll closing from all sides.

Cook on a hot griddle until it is crisp on both sides. Mix everything for the sauce and beat in a blender.

Cut the rolls into half place diagonally on a serving plate with the sauce drizzled on it or served on the side.

BURRITO

Ingredients :
For the dough :
- 1 ½ cups wheat flour
- ½ cup plain flour (maida)
- 3 tsp oil
- ½ tsp salt

For the stuffing :
- 1 cup boiled kidney beans mashed.
- 1 chopped onion
- 2 tbsp tomato puree
- 2 tbsp tomato ketchup
- 2 tbsp ghee
- 2 tbsp butter
- Salt to taste

For garnishing :
- ½ cup sour cream
- 1 cup cheddar cheese grated
- Sliced jalapenos
- Hot sauce
- ½ cup chopped spring onions

Let's Cook :

To make the dough, mix all the ingredients and make a soft dough. Roll out into thin rounds and cook on both sides on a griddle without any oil.

Heat ghee and butter together in a pan and fry the onions till golden brown. Add the mashed beans, ketchup, tomato puree, salt and cook till the colours darkens, mashing the mixture as it cooks. Remove from heat and keep aside.

To serve take a tortilla and put some bean filling towards the bottom. Sprinkle with spring onions, grated cheese, hot sauce, jalapenos and sour cream.

Roll lightly and serve.

QUINOA BLACK BEAN TACOS WITH CREAMY AVOCADO SAUCE

Ingredients :

Avocado sauce :

- 1 large avocado, sliced into long strips
- 1-2 medium limes juiced
- 1 medium jalapeno, deseeded, membranes removed and roughly chopped
- 1 handful fresh cilantro
- ¼ tsp salt

Quinoa and Black Bean filling :

- 1 tbsp olive oil
- 1 cup chopped red onion
- 2 large garlic cloves minced
- 3 tbsp tomato paste
- 1 tsp ground cumin
- ½ tsp ground chilli powder
- ½ cup uncooked quinoa
- 1 cup water
- 1 can black beans or 1 ½ cups cooked beans, rinsed and drained
- Salt to taste
- Freshly ground black pepper to taste.

Everything else :

- 6 to 8 small, round corn tortillas 1 ½ cups roughly chopped lettuce, pickled jalapenos.
- Crumbled feta cheese.

Let's Cook :

To make the filling, warm the olive oil over medium heat sauté the onion and garlic with a dash of salt for 4-5 min., until the onions turn translucent. Add the tomato paste, cumin powder and chilli powder and sauté stirring continuously.

Add the rinsed quinoa and water. Bring the mixture to boil, then cover the pot and cook for 15 mins. on a low flame. Remove from heat and allow it to rest covered for 5 mins. Drain off any excess liquid. Add drained black beans, salt, pepper, cover and set aside.

To make the avocado sauce : Simply combine the ingredients in a food processor. Blend well and season with salt.

In a large skillet over medium heat, warm the tortillas, flipping halfway. Wrap the warmed tortillas until ready to serve.

To assemble the tacos, spread quinoa and black bean filling down the centre of the tortilla, then top with avocado cream, a handful of chopped lettuce, pickled jalapenos and crumbled feta cheese and serve.

CUCUMBER CREAM CANAPES

Ingredients :
- 1 cucumber
- 5 tbsp cream cheese
- 10 thin white bread slices
- 3 tbsp parsley chopped
- Salt & white pepper to taste

Let's Cook :

Cut the cucumber into ¼ inch slices. With a small cookie cutter cut out 20 cucumber hearts or any other shape you desire.

Spread the cream cheese on the bread cut out 20 canape hearts with a large pastry cutter.

Spread parsley an a flat dish and dip edges of the canapés in the parsley.

Top canapés with cucumber hearts and sprinkle with salt and pepper serve chilled.

CURRIES

VEGAN THAI CURRY VEGETABLES

Ingredients :
- One can coconut milk
- ½ cup vegetable stock
- 4 tsp soy sauce
- 4 tsp brown sugar
- 6 tbsp Thai green curry paste
- ½ cup diced onion
- 2/3 cup diced red bell pepper
- 2/3 cup diced zucchini
- 2/3 cup diced sweet potato
- 1 cup green beans cut into 1 ½ inch lengths
- 2/3 cup diced Asian eggplant (Bringal)
- 1 lime
- 8 large basil leaves

Let's Cook :

Open the can of coconut milk without shaking it. Spoon 6 tbsp cream from the top of the can into a sauce pan. Pour the remaining cream into a medium bowl and mix well.

In a another bowl combine vegetable stock, soy sauce and brown sugar. Stir until the sugar is dissolved.

Place sauce pan of coconut cream over medium high heat until it begins to bubble. Add Thai green curry paste. Stir continuously about 3 mins. Add onion, red bell pepper, zucchini, sweet potato, green beans and egg plant. Stir until vegetables are hot, 2-3 min. Stir in coconut milk and cook until the vegetables are tender.

Add the soy sauce mixture and lime juice to taste. Add ¼ cup water if the curry seems too thick.

To serve place the curry in a warm serving bowl and garnish with basil leaves.

VEGETABLE MAKHANWALA (ASSORTED VEGETABLES IN CREAMY GRAVY)

Ingredients :

- Green peas ½ cup
- Carrot chopped – 2 medium
- French beans chopped – 4
- Green bell peppers chopped – 1 medium
- Cauliflower cut into florets – ½ medium
- Baby potatoes peeled – 4
- Butter – 4 tbsp
- Cumin seeds – ½ tsp
- Salt to taste
- Whole dry red chillies – 2
- Red chilli paste – ½ tsp
- Tomato ketchup – 1 tbsp
- Tomato puree boiled – 1 cup
- Fresh cream – ½ cup
- Kasoor methi – 1 tbsp
- Cashew nuts – 10
- Almonds – 10
- Ginger – 1 inch pc
- Garlic 5-6 cloves

Let's Cook :

First heat 1/3 cup milk and soak cashews and almonds in hot milk for 30 minutes. While cashews and almonds are soaking rinse and chop the vegetables. Heat 1 tbsp butter and sauté the veggies on low heat till they are almost cooked. Take out and keep aside.

Take a blender, add tomatoes, ginger, garlic, soaked nuts and make a smooth paste. Heat 2 tbsp butter in a pan, add cumin seeds and broken red chillies and let them splatter. Add tomato puree, keep on stirring and sautéing paste till you see fat leaving the sides of the pan. Add red chilli paste, ketchup, garam masala, salt and mix well.

Add the fried veggies and crushed kasoori methi, stir for a minute and then add fresh cream. Stir so that cream mixes very well with the gravy.

Switch off the flame veg makhanwala is ready to serve. While serving garnish with cilantro and fresh cream. Serve hot with Roti, paratha, naan etc.

HARIALI MATAR (GREEN PEAS GRAVY)

Ingredients :

- 2 cups chopped cilantro
- 1 pc ginger
- 4 cloves garlic
- 3 green chillies chopped
- 1 tbsp lemon juice
- 2 tsp oil
- 1 tbsp cumin seeds
- A pinch of asafetida
- 2 cups boiled green peas
- Salt to taste
- ¼ cup low fat milk
- ¼ cup grated paneer (cottage cheese)

Let's Cook :

Make a green masala paste by grinding cilantro, ginger, garlic, green chillies and lemon juice. Heat the oil in a pan. Add cumin seeds first. When the seeds crackle, add asafoetida. Add green peas and sauté an a medium flame for 3-4 mins, add the prepared green paste and salt and cook for 3-4 mins. Then add the milk and mix well and cook for another 2 minutes. Just before serving add the paneer and mix well and serve hot.

STUFFED OKRA

Ingredients :
- 1 tbsp raw mango powder (Amchur)
- 2 tbsp cilantro
- 1 tsp Red chilli powder
- 1 tsp turmeric powder
- 1 tsp cumin powder
- Salt to taste
- 500 gms okra
- 2-3 tbsp oil

Let's Cook :

Wash okra in water, drain and then wipe them dry with a kitchen towel. Keep aside.

In a bowl take all the dry masala powder. Add salt and mix all the masalas together. Keep aside.

Trim the head and the base of okra's with a knife. Give a slit, stuff the masala in the okra one by one with a small spoon.

Heat oil in a wok. Add stuffed okras and stir gently. If any masalas remains you can add it to the wok. Let it cook on a low flame. Stir in between. Once well cooked serve hot.

SCHEZWAN COTTAGE CHEESE CURRY

Ingredients :

- ½ cup schezwan sauce
- 200 gms cubed cottage cheese (paneer)
- ½ cup cubed bell pepper
- 1 onion finely sliced
- 1 tomato finely chopped
- Salt to taste
- Oil 2 tbsp
- 1 tsp cornflour dissolved in 1 tbsp milk

Let's Cook :

Heat a wok and add oil, add sliced onions and sauté till golden. In the meanwhile add the paneer pieces in boiling water and keep closed. Add tomatoes and cook till mushy. Add bell peppers and sauté till they shrink a bit but colour should not change.

Next add the paneer and sauté for 5 mins. Then add the schezwan sauce and coat it well over the veggies and paneer. Add ½ cup water, salt and allow the gravy to thicken. Add cornflour dissolved in milk and cook for 5 minutes and serve hot.

FRENCH BEANS DUMPLINGS IN A SWEET AND SAVOURY GRAVY

Ingredients :

For dumplings

- 3 tbsp besan (chickpea flour)
- 1 tbsp wheat flour
- ½ tsp red chilli powder
- ¼ tsp turmeric powder
- ¼ tsp asafoetida
- ¼ tsp carom seeds
- ½ tsp oil
- Salt to taste

Other ingredients

- 2 cups chopped French beans
- 2 tsp oil
- 1 tsp carom seeds
- ¼ tsp asafoetida
- ½ tsp red chilli powder
- ¼ tsp sugar
- Salt to taste
- Juice of 1 lemon

Let's Cook :

For dumplings : combine all the ingredients in a bowl and knead into a semi soft dough using water. Divide the dough into small equal portions. Press each portion with your thumb to make a circular mini dumpling. Keep aside.

Heat oil in a pan. Add carom seeds, asafoetida and sauté. Add chopped French beans, 1 cup of water, red chilli powder, sugar, salt, lemon juice and cook an medium flame for 5 minutes or till the beans are almost done. Add dumplings and simmer for another 10-12 minutes while stirring occasionally.

Serve hot garnished with cilantro, 1 tsp of clarified butter and lemon juice.

GREEN PEAS AND FENUGREEK LEAVES COOKED IN A CREAMY GRAVY (METHI MUTTER MALAI)

Ingredients :
- Green peas – 1 cup
- Fenugreek leaves (Methi) 1 bunch finely chopped
- Fresh cream – ½ cup
- One tomato pureed
- Cumin seeds – ½ tsp
- Turmeric powder – a pinch
- Green chilli paste – 1 tbsp
- Butter – 1 tbsp
- Milk if required
- Salt to taste

For paste :
- Onion – 1
- Green chilli – 1-2
- Almonds and cashew nuts – 8 – 10
- Poppy seeds – 1 tbsp
- Curd – 1 tbsp
- Ginger – ½" pc
- Cloves – 3
- Cinnamon – ½" stick
- Cardamom – 1

Let's Cook :

Roast all the ingredients for paste and add curd and make a fine paste and keep aside.

Rinse fenugreek leaves. Heat butter in a pan, add cumin seeds, green chilli paste, turmeric powder, tomato puree, paste and let it cook for 3-4 minutes.

Add boiled green peas, fenugreek leaves and fresh cream. Add milk to get desired consistency boil for 5 minutes until gravy thickens and ingredients are cooked well. Serve hot garnished with fresh cream and serve with Roti, nan, bread etc.

BITTERGOURD RINGS

Ingredients :
- Bittergourd finely sliced – 2
- Chickpea flour – 2 tbsp
- Rice flour – 2 tbsp
- Red chilli powder – ½ tsp
- Garam masala – ½ tsp
- Amchur powder (Dry mango powder) ½ tsp
- Chat masala – ½ tsp

Let's Cook :

Finely slice the bittergourd into roundals and place in a bowl. Add salt and turmeric powder, mix and keep aside.

Heat oil in a pan. Rinse the marinated bittergourd with water and remove in another bowl. Add red chilli powder, garam masala, salt, raw mango powder and chat masala and mix well.

Add chickpea flour and rice flour and mix well. Deep fry the bittergourd in hot oil till crisp. Drain on absorbent paper. Garnish with chat masala and serve.

SPICY CUCUMBER

Ingredients :

- 1 English cucumber
- ¼ cup thinly sliced onion
- 1 green onion chopped
- 2 garlic cloves minced
- 2 tbsp soy sauce
- 2 tsp hot pepper flakes
- 2 tsp sesame oil
- 2 tsp sesame seeds
- 1 tsp sugar (optional)

Let's Cook :

Cut the cucumber lengthwise in half and cut diagonally into thin slices. Put the cucumber into a large bowl. Add the onion, green onion, garlic, soy sauce, hot pepper flakes, sesame oil, sesame seeds and sugar.

Mix it well with a spoon until the sugar is well dissolved.

Serve as a side dish for rice, noodles or BBQ.

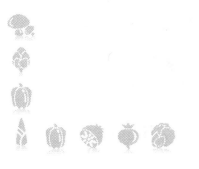

PANEER LABABDAR (COTTAGE CHEESE DUMPLINGS IN HOT RED GRAVY)

Ingredients :
- 1 cup cottage cheese cubed.
- ½ tsp cumin seeds
- 1 tsp coriander seeds roasted and crushed
- 3 whole red chillies crushed
- ½ tsp kasuri methi
- ½ cup finely chopped onions
- 1 ½ tsp ginger garlic paste
- ¼ tsp turmeric powder
- 1 ½ cup chopped tomatoes
- ½ cup milk
- ¼ tsp cornflour
- ¼ tsp garam masala (All spice powder)
- 1 tsp oil
- Salt to taste

Let's Cook :

Heat oil in a pan. Add cumin seeds, coriander seeds, ground chillies, kasuri methi, onions and sauté till the onions turn light brown in colour.

Add the ginger-garlic paste, turmeric powder, tomatoes with 4 tbsp of water and cook till fat separates from the sides.

Cool the mixture and puree to a smooth paste and transfer in a non-stick pan.

Dissolve the cornflour in the milk and add it to the gravy and simmer for 3-4 min.

Add the cubed cottage cheese, garam masala and salt and mix well. Serve hot with Roti, Nan, Paratha etc.

RICE

MEXICAN RICE

Ingredients :

- Rice soaked & drained – 1 ½ cups
- Tomatoes – 2 large
- Olive oil – 2 tbsp
- Red bell pepper – 1 medium
- Whole dry red chillies – 2 – 3
- Garlic – 6 cloves
- Onion sliced – 1 large
- Salt to taste
- Water – 2 ½ cups
- Carrots thickly grated – 2 medium

Let's Cook :

Heat 1 tbsp olive oil in a pan. Add red capsicum, dry red chillies, tomatoes and sauté on high heat till slightly charred.

Cool and grind to a smooth paste. Heat the remaining olive oil in another pan, add onion and saute till light golden. Add rice and saute.

Add the paste, water and salt and mix. Add carrots and mix. Cook till done serve hot.

LAPAY (JAGGERY RICE)

Ingredients :

- 1 cup par boiled rice
- 1 ¼ cup grated jaggery
- 4 tbsp ghee (clarified butter)
- Cinnomin stick 1 pc
- Cloves – 2-3
- Bay leaves – 2
- 2 pinches of saffron strands
- Dissolved in 2 tbsp warm milk
- 2 tbsp almond slices
- 2 tbsp chopped cashew nuts
- 1 tbsp cardamom powder

Let's Cook :

First take the jiggery and soak it in water and allow it to boil till it dissolves completely. Pick, clean and rinse the rice. Soak the rice for 15-20 minutes. In a pan add the rice and 2 cups of water and allow it to cook till the rice is partially cooked.

Mix dissolved jaggery with partially cooked rice. Add ghee and stir it gently. Now add cloves, bay leaves, raisins and saffron soaked in milk. Stir this very gently with the rice mixture. Now close the lid and allow it to cook. Stir in between. Cook till all the water burns out and rice gets completely cooked. If required you can add water to the rice for cooking.

When the rice is completely cooked transfer it into a serving dish. Garnish the cooked jaggery rice with roasted almonds slices, chopped cashew nuts and cardamom powder. Add 1 tbsp clarified butter (ghee) on it and serve hot.

THAI FRAGRANT RICE

Ingredients :
- Thai Jasmine Rice – 1 cup
- Spring Onion with greens – 1 cup
- Coconut milk – 2 cups
- Lemon rind grated – 2 tsp
- Lemon grass roots – 1"
- Ginger – 1" pieces
- Salt to taste
- Vegetable stock

Let's Cook :

Trim the spring onions greens and reserve. Roughly chop the stems and quarter the bulbs.

Heat a deep non-stick pan, add the drained rice, coconut milk, spring onion bulbs and stems, vegetable stock and lemon rind.

Slice lemon grass root and add slice ginger, salt and mix. Cook till the rice is done. Chop spring onion greens and garnish the rice.

COCONUT RICE

Ingredients :

- Scraped coconut – 1 cup
- Cooked rice – 2 cups
- Coconut oil – 2-3 tbsp
- Mustard seeds – ½ tsp
- Dried red chillies broken – 2
- Splitted black gram – 1 tsp
- Curry leaves – 6-8
- Ginger finely chopped – 1 tbsp
- Green chillies broken – 1
- Peanuts deep fried – ¼ cup
- Salt to taste
- Fresh coriander leaves – 2-3 tbsp
- Freshly ground black pepper – 2 tbsp
- Splitted Bengal gram – 1 tbsp

Let's Cook :

Heat oil in a wok. Add mustard seeds and let them splutter. Add red chillies, splitted Bengal gram and black gram and sauté till it turns light brown.

Add curry leaves, ginger and green chilli. Mix and add grated coconut and sauté for a while on low heat. Add peanuts and mix. Add rice and mix lightly. Add salt, pepper powder and stir lightly.

Serve hot garnished with coriander leaves and deep fried coconut slices.

KASHMIRI PULAO

Ingredients :

- Cottage cheese – ½" cubes – 250 g
- Basmati rice – 1 ½ cups
- Saffron – few strands
- Oil for deep frying
- Sliced onion – 1 cup
- Cardamom – 3
- Bay leaves – 3
- Cloves – 3
- Cinnamon – 2" pc
- Dry ginger powder – ½ tsp
- Fennel seeds – 1 tsp
- Asafoetida – ¼ tsp
- Clarified butter (ghee) – 3 tbsp
- Cumin seeds – 1 tsp
- Raisins – 10-12
- Cashew nuts halved – 8
- Salt to taste

Let's Cook :

Soak the rice in 3 cups of water for half on hour. Drain, soak saffron in 2 tsp warm milk. Heat oil in a wok and deep fry the sliced onions till golden and crisp. Drain on the absorbent paper.

Bring 4 ½ cups of water. Add cardamoms, bay leaves, cloves, cinnamon, dry ginger powder, fennel seeds, asafoetida and salt to the water and boil, however heat and simmer for 15-20 mins or till reduced to 3 cups. Remove from heat and strain the stock.

Discard the spices. Heat ghee in a deep pan. Add cumin seeds and cardamoms. When the cumin seeds change colour add soaked rice and the stock. Bring to a boil, lower heat, cover and cook till the rice is almost done.

Gently stir in the cubed cottage cheese, raisins and cashew nuts sprinkle soaked saffron and fried onions over the rice. Cook on dum for another 8 to 10 minutes or in a microwave oven covered with a foil paper. Serve hot with raita, papad and lemon pickle.

YOGURT RICE

Ingredients :
- Cooked rice – 2 cups
- Curd – 1 cup
- Milk – ¼ cup
- Oil – 1 tbsp
- Salt to taste
- Finely chopped green chillies – 1 tbsp
- Splitted black gram – ½ tsp
- Mustard seeds – ½ tsp
- Splitted bengal gram – 1 tsp
- Asafoetida – ¼ tsp
- Curry leaves – 10-15
- Whole red chillies – 1
- Pomegranate seeds, coriander leaves.

Let's Cook :

Heat oil in a deep pan. Place rice in a separate bowl, add milk, yogurt and salt and mix well. Chop green chilli and add to rice. Add black gram, Bengal gram mustard seeds, asafetida, curry leaves, whole red chilli to the pan and let the seeds splutter.

Add the tempering to rice and mix well. Chill in refrigerator. Serve chilled garnished with coriander leaves and pomegranate seeds.

VEGETABLE HYDERABADI BIRYANI

Ingredients :

- Basmati rice – 1 ½ cups
- Potatoes – 2 large
- Carrots cubed – 3
- French beans ½" pc – 5-6
- Cauliflower florets – 1 cup
- Salt to taste
- Saffron – 4-5 strands soaked in milk
- Onion thinly sliced – 4
- Oil to deep fry
- Yogurt – ½ cup
- Biryani masala – 3 tbsp
- Ginger-garlic paste – 1 tbsp
- Clarified butter – 4 tbsp
- Mint leaves chopped – 2 tbsp
- Coriander leaves chopped – 2 tbsp
- Cashew nuts – 5
- Almonds – 10
- Raisins – 2 tbsp
- Wheat flour dough to seal the pan

Let's Cook :

Pick, rinse and soak the rice in 3 cups of water for half an hour, drain. Add 4 cups of water and salt. Bring to boil and cook till the rice is ¾ th done. Drain excess water and let it cool. Par boil potatoes, carrots, beans, cauliflower into two cups of salted water, drain and keep aside. Heat sufficient oil in a deep pan and deep fry onions till golden brown. Beat yogurt, add biryani masala, half of the fried onions, ginger-garlic paste and par boiled veggies. Allow it to marinate for an hour.

Heat clarified butter in a wok add the marinated veggies and sauté for 2-3 mins.

Pre-heat the oven to 180⁰ C. Transfer the veggies into oven safe deep bowl. Layer the rice over the cooked veggies. Sprinkle the remaining biryani masala, mint leaves, coriander leaves and the remaining fried onions. Garnish with cashew nuts, almonds and raisins.

Sprinkle saffron milk, place a moist cloth on the top. Cover with a lid and seal with dough.

Put the sealed bowl in the pre-heated oven and cook at 180⁰C for 15-20 mins.

Serve hot with raita.

TRIPLE SCHEZWAN FRIED RICE

Ingredients :

- Boiled rice 2 cup
- Boiled noodles 1 cup
- Onion finely chopped – 1
- Red and green bell pepper – 1 each
- Finely chopped
- Ginger chopped 1 tsp
- Garlic chopped – 2 tsp
- Schezwan sauce – 2 ½ tbsp
- Soy sauce – 2 tsp
- Spring onion chopped – ½ cup
- Tomato sauce – 1 tbsp
- Vinegar – 1 tsp
- Salt for taste
- Black pepper powder – 1 tsp
- Red chilli sauce – 1 tbsp

Let's Cook :

Heat a wok put in 2 tsp oil to heat, add onion, garlic, bell peppers and sauté it. Then add red chilli sauce, schezwan sauce, Soy sauce, tomato sauce, vinegar, salt and black pepper powder.

Then add boiled rice, boiled noodles and mix very well. Serve hot garnished with spring onions. Serve hot with Manchurian of your choice.

BAKED RICE

Ingredients :

- 2 ½ cups boiled rice.
- 300 g cubed & par boiled potatoes
- 1 onion chopped
- 1 kg fresh spinach boiled and pureed
- 2 cloves garlic chopped
- 2 tsp dried oregano
- 3 cups white sauce
- 1 cup grated cheddar cheese
- Salt and pepper to taste

Let's Cook :

Mix the rice, potatoes and white sauce in a bowl. Add oregano, salt and pepper and keep aside. Heat oil in a pan and sauté the onions along with the garlic. Add the spinach, salt and pepper and make a thick sauce.

Take a deep oven proof dish and spread the spinach sauce at the bottom.

Then layer with the rice and potato mixture. Spread the cheese and bake. Serve immediately.

ROTIS AND BREADS

METHI THEPLA (INDIAN FLAT BREAD WITH FENUGREEK LEAVES)

Ingredients :
- 1 cup fenugreek leaves
- 1 cup whole wheat flour
- ¼ cup chickpea flour
- Ginger 1" pc grated
- 3 green chillies finely chopped
- ½ tsp red chilli powder
- 1 tsp jeera powder
- ½ tsp coriander powder
- Salt to taste
- Sesame seeds – 1 tbsp
- Yogurt 4-5 tbsp
- Oil – 2 tbsp
- Oil for roasting theplas

Let's Cook :

Rince 1 cup fenugreek leaves very well in water. The drain them and chop finely. Keep aside in a mixing bowl take both the flour add all spices, fenugreek leaves and oil, mix well. Add yogurt and knead the dough very well. If required add water for kneading. Make medium size balls and roll the theplas.

On a hot griddle place the thepla and roast it with oil till golden brown.

Serve methi thepla with yogurt and pickle.

COTTAGE CHEESE KULCHA (INDIAN FLAT BREAD)

Ingredients :
- All purpose flour (maida) – 2 cups
- Salt – ½ tsp
- Soda-bi-carb – ¼ tsp
- Sugar – 1 tsp
- Milk – ½ cup
- Yogurt – 1 tbsp

Stuffing :
- Grated cottage cheese – 200 gms
- Salt to taste
- Red chilli powder – 1 tsp
- Chat masala – ½ tsp
- Coriander leaves – 1 tbsp

Let's Cook :

Take maida in a bowl. Add salt, yogurt, soda, sugar and milk and knead into a soft dough. Cover with a damp cloth and rest for 1 hour.

Make balls from the dough and rest for another 5-10 minutes.

Take cottage cheese in a bowl, add salt, red chilli powder and chat masala and mix well.

Roll each balls in to a small puri, place a portion of cottage cheese mixture and roll into a ball again.

Pat each ball into a round kulcha and place on a baking tray. Rub a little water on the surface and sprinkle some red chilli powder. Bake in the pre-heated oven till golden brown.

Serve hot with butter an each side.

DRIED FRUIT LOAF

Ingredients :

- 600 gms all purpose flour
- 200 gms whole meat flour
- 200 gms fine semolina
- 60 ml grape seed oil
- 1 tbsp honey
- 15 gms salt
- 800 ml water
- 2 sachets dry yeast
- 200 gms chopped apricots
- 200 gms chopped dates
- 200 gms sultanas
- 200 gms chopped walnuts

Let's Cook :

Add a spoon of honey to warm water. Add 2 sachets of yeast and stir well and keep aside mix both the flour and the semolina in a large bowl and add the yeast mixture, add grape seed oil and add the chopped dried fruits. Mix well with a beater for about 5 minutes.

Knead by hand until smooth and silky. Cover and allow to rise for about 4 hours. Knead into a roll and divide dough into two loaves place into lined baking tins. Allow to rise for about 45 minutes or double in size.

Pre-heat the oven to 180°C and bake for about 50 minutes. Remove from oven and cut into slices.

Fruit loaf is best eaten fresh but can be frozen wrapped in foil.

CHOCLATE PARATHA

Ingredients :
- Wheat flour – 1 cup
- Method chocolate – ½ cup
- Walnuts crushed – 1 tbsp
- Almonds crushed – 1 tbsp
- Ghee – 1 tbsp
- Milk as required

Let's Cook :
Melt the chocolate in double boiler. Take the wheat flour and add melted chocolate, walnuts, Almonds knead it into a dough using milk. Make small balls and roll out parathas. Cook on a griddle applying clarified butter on both sides.

Serve hot.

PESHAWARI NAAN

Ingredients :

- 4 cups all purpose flour
- 1 tsp baking powder
- ½ tsp soda-bi-caab
- 1 tsp salt
- 2 tsp sugar
- 2 tbsp yogurt
- 1 cup milk
- 2 tbsp oil
- Butter as required
- 2 tbsp finely chopped cashew nuts
- 2 tbsp finely chopped almonds
- 2 tbsp pistachios chopped
- 2 tbsp coarsely crushed fennel seeds.

Let's Cook :

Sieve all purpose flour, baking powder and soda-bi-carb. Add salt, sugar, yogurt, milk, oil and butter. Knead a dough Dough should be very soft.

Pre-heat the oven. Roll Naan to oval shape. Sprinkle fennel seeds, cashewnuts, pistas & almonds. Apply little butter and cook till done.

CHOCLATE ZUCCHINI BREAD

Ingredients :

- 1 ½ cups shredded Zucchini
- 1 cup whole wheat flour
- ½ cup cocoa powder
- 1 tsp baking soda
- ½ tsp baking powder
- ¼ tsp salt
- ¼ tsp ground all spice
- ¼ cup oil
- ¼ cup unsweetened apple sauce
- ½ cup white sugar
- ½ cup brown sugar
- 6-8 tbsp butter milk
- 1 tsp vanilla extract
- ¼ cup semi sweet, chocolate chips

Let's Cook :

Pre-heat the oven to 180°C for 15 mins. Lightly grease loof pan and also line it up with a piece of parchment paper to enable easy removal of the loaf from the pan.

In a large mixing bowl combine flour, cocoa powder, salt and spice, leaveners.

In another medium size bowl beat together the oil, applesauce, both the sugars, buttermilk and vanilla extract. Fold the grated zucchini. To this add the flour mixture and beat it. Stir in the chocolate chips.

Transfer the batter to the prepared loaf pan and bake it between 40-45 minutes or until a tooth pick inserted comes out clean.

Transfer the pan from the oven and place it an a wire rack. Remove the bread from the pan after 10 minutes and let it cool completely before you can slice it.

IRISH BROWN BREAD

Ingredients :

- 1 ½ cups all purpose flour
- 1 ½ cups whole wheat flour
- ½ cup quick oats
- ½ cup wheat germ
- 1 ½ tsp baking soda
- ¾ tsp salt
- 1 ¾ cups buttermilk
- 2 tbsp honey

Let's Cook :

Preheat oven to 180°C for 15 minutes. In a bowl combine all purpose flour, wheat flour, oats, wheat germ, baking soda and salt.

In a small bowl, mix buttermilk with honey. Add liquid ingredients to flour mixture. Stir to combine.

Turn dough out on to floured surface and shape it. Place on a greased baking tray and bake for 30-35 minutes or until the bread sounds hollow when you tap it. Let it cool before slicing.

Serve the bread slices with your favorite jam.

DESERTS

INDIAN RED ROSE FUDGE

Ingredients :
- 250 g Indian Red rose petals
- 250 g Khoya grated
- 300 g Sugar
- Clarified butter as required
- Rose essence 1 tbsp

Let's Cook :

Roast washed and crushed rose petals in a pan. Take another pan and roast khoya and add roasted petals, also add sugar and stir well. When sugar melts take it down from the flame and add essence. Invert the mixer in a greased plate and flatten it.

When it cools cut into pieces garnished with rose petals.

GULAB JAMUN MOUSSE

Ingredients :
- Gulab jamuns – 12 small
- Milk chocolate chopped – ½ cup
- Fresh cream – 1 cup
- White chocolate chopped – ½ cup
- Whipping cream – 1 ½ cups
- Few rid rose petals
- Gulkand – 1 tbsp
- Rose water – 1 tsp
- Pistachios for garnishing

Let's Cook :

Heat a non-stick pan, add milk chocolate, cream and stir till it melts. Add white chocolate and stir till it melts and all the ingredients blend well. Take care that mixture do not get too hot.

Pass the mixture through the sieve and keep in refrigerator and cool it.

Place the whipped cream in a bowl. Add gulkand chop a few rose petals finely and add rose water and the chocolate cream mixture and mix everything lightly.

Put a gulab jamun in each of the 6 glasses. Put the mousse over the gulab jamun in each glass and pot the glasses lightly so that mousse goes down right to the bottom.

Place a gulab jamun on the top of the mousse in each glass. Place a few pistachios on one side and a whole rose petal on the other. Chill in the refrigerator till well set and serve.

CHOCLATE WALNUT FUDGE

Ingredients :
- Chopped walnuts – ½ cup
- Dark chocolate – 100 g
- Unsalted butter – 4 tbsp
- Condensed milk – 400 g
- Vanilla essence – ½ tsp
- Grated khoya – ½ cup

Let's Cook :

Grease a baking tray and keep aside. Heat a pan, add butter and allow it to melt. Add dark chocolate and stir till it melts. Mix condensed milk and cook for 2-3 minutes. Add chopped walnuts, khoya, Vanilla essence and mix well. Transfer the mixture to the greased tray and spread evenly and cool in refrigerator before cutting into pieces.

Serve chilled.

INSTANT PINEAPPLE CAKE

Ingredients :
- 1 cup maida (All purpose flour)
- 1 cup milk powder
- 1 cup sugar
- ½ cup clarified butter
- 1 tsp baking powder
- ½ tsp pineapple essence
- Yellow food colour few drops
- Tooty fruity – ½ cup
- Milk – 1 glass

Let's Cook :

Mix all the ingredients well. Grease the microwave safe bowl and pour the mixture. Mixture should be very thin. Garnish with Tooty fruity keep on a microwave mode for 8-10 minutes. Check it with a knife. If it is ready take it out. Preheat the microwave on grill mode for 3 minutes. Then keep the cake for 2-3 minutes for top browning, cool it and cut into pieces and serve.

ALMOND SHEERA (HALWA)

Ingredients :

- Almond powder – 3/4 cup
- Wheat flour – ¼ cup
- Ghee (clarified butter) ½ cup
- Sugar – 1 cup
- Cashewnuts – 5-6
- Kismis 5-6 (Raisins)
- Saffron few strands
- Milk – 1 cup
- Hot water - 1 cup
- Cardamom powder – ¼ tsp

Let's Cook :

Heat clarified butter in a pan. Add wheat flour and roast till golden brown. Add almond powder and roast. Add milk, water and cook till all the water dissolves completely. Add saffron soaked in milk, chopped cashewnuts, raisins and sugar and cook till sheera leaves the sides of the pan. Add cardamom powder and mix well. Serve hot.

INSTANT JALEBI

Ingredients :

- Self Rising flour – 1 cup
- Citric acid – ¼ tsp
- Yellow food colour – 1 tbsp
- Sugar – 1 ½ cup
- Chasni – 1 thread
- Clarified butter for deep fry

Let's Cook :

In a bowl add flour, food colour, citric acid and make a batter using water.

In a another pan add sugar and water and boil. Cook till it forms 1 thread chasni.

Fill the batter in jalebi maker and fry the jalebis in hot ghee till crisp. Add the jalebis in sugar syrup. Soak for 2 minutes and drain it and serve hot.

PAAN KULFI

Ingredients :

- 1/8 cup gulkand
- 1 tbsp good quality meetha pan chutney (sween beetel leaf chutney)
- 1 small beetel leaves chopped
- ¼ tsp cardamons powder
- 2 ½ cup unsweetened condensed milk
- ½ cup sweetened condensed milk
- ½ cup whipping cream
- Rose petal

Let's Cook :

Combine gulkand, beetel leaves, and paan chutney very well. Put both milk and cream in blender and blend until smooth. Add in this mixture cardamom powder and paan mixture, mix very well. Pour this mixture into kulfi or popsicle moulds. Keep them in the freezer till set Garnish with sweet and colourful fennel seeds and rose petal and then serve.

APPLE ENCHILADA DESSERT

Ingredients :
- 1 cap apple pie filling
- 6 flour tortillas
- 1 tsp ground cinnamon
- 1/3 cup margarine
- ½ cup white sugar
- ½ cup brown sugar
- ½ cup water

Let's Cook :
Pre-heat oven to 180°C spoon fruit evenly onto all tortillas sprinkle with cinnamon. Roll up tortillas and place seam side down on lightly greased baking pan.

Bring margarine, sugars and water to boil in a medium sauce pan. Reduce heat and simmer, stirring constantly for 3 minutes.

Pour sauce evenly over tortillas, sprinkle with extra cinnamon on top. Bake in preheated oven for 20 minutes.

Remove and serve cut into 2 pieces.

BANANA SPRING ROLLS

Ingredients :
- Oil for frying
- 2 bananas
- 2 tbsp salted butter
- 4 tsp sugar
- Cinnamon to taste
- Icing sugar to serve
- 4 spring roll wrappers

Let's Cook :

Heat oil in a deep pan. Slice each banana in half lengthwise. Then slice each piece into half to get 4 pc in total.

Melt butter in microwave for about 20-30 sec. stir until completely melted. Add bananas, sugar and cinnamon to the melted butter. Mix well.

Place quartered bananas on the spring roll wrapper and roll up and lightly oil the end to seel place the roll seam side down on a plate while the oil heats up.

Deep fry the rolls until golden brown turning occasionally. Remove from oil and drain. Finally dust with icing sugar and cinnamon and serve.

THAI LIGHT ORANGE BLOSSOM

Ingredients :
- 2 cups water
- 1 cup sugar
- 3 whole star anise
- 2 tsp orange flower water
- 6 large oranges
- Fresh mint

Let's Cook :

Combine water, sugar and star anise in a medium sauce pan. Stir over medium heat until sugar dissolved. Simmer until liquid is reduced to 1 cup.

Remove from heat and stir in orange flower water. Chill until cold. Discard anise.

Cut, peel and deseed oranges with knife. Slice oranges. Set in bowls spoon syrup over. Top with fresh mint and serve chilled.

BERRY SAUCE WITH GREEK YOGURT

Ingredients :

For Sauce

- 2 cups mixed berries (Raspberries, blue berries and black berries)
- ¼ cup sugar
- 1 tbsp lemon juice
- 1 tsp vanilla extract
- 1 tbsp butter
- ½ cup water

For sweet greek yogurt

- 2 cup strained thick yogurt
- 1 tbsp honey
- ½ tsp vanilla extract
- Mixed berries, mint leaves for garnishing

Let's Cook :

In a sauce pan add berries, sugar, lemon juice, vanilla extract and water and bring it to the boil on high flame. Then add butter and stir it again.

Switch off the flame and let it cool down till warm, then blend but do not make fine puree.

In a mixing bowl add yogurt, honey and vanilla extract and mix it well keep aside.

Take a serving glasses, add ¼ part berry sauce, add sweet greek yogurt over the sauce, use long tooth pick and make patterns as per your choice.

Garnish with mixed berries and mint leaves.

Serve fresh.

SUKHADI (GUR PAPDI)

Ingredients :

- 1 cup wheat flour
- ½ cup jaggery grated (Gur)
- ¾ cup clarified butter
- 1 tsp cardamom powder
- 1 tbsp sliced almonds
- 1 tbsp fennel seeds
- 2 tbsp fresh cream

Let's Cook :

Heat clarified butter in a pan. Add flour and roast till golden brown. Turn off the gas. Add jaggery, cardamom powder and mix well till all the jaggery melts. Add fresh cream and mix and pour in a greased baking dish and flatten it. Cut into triangles garnish with almond slices, fennel seeds crushed, cardamom powder and serve.

CASSATA SANDESH

Ingredients :

- 150 gm paneer (cottage cheese)
- 4 tsp milk powder
- 4 tsp condensed milk
- 3 tsp powdered sugar
- ½ cup milk
- 1 tsp cornflour
- 1 tsp clarified butter
- 2-3 drops each (vanilla essence)
- Rose essence, pineapple essence, mix fruit essence)
- 1-2 pinch each (Red, yellow, green food colour)
- 2-3 tsp green, red, yellow tutty fruity

Let's Cook :

In a blender add pancer, milk powder, condensed milk, sugar, cornflour, milk and clarified butter and blend to a smooth paste. Then take this paste in a pan and cook an medium flame stirring continuously till it leaves the pan and form a ball.

Remove from heat and allow it to cool knead well and make four parts. In first part add vanilla essence, and all the three colour tutty fruit and mix and keep aside.

In second part add rose essence, red food colour and green tutty fruity and mix.

In third part add pineapple essence, yellow food colour and red tutty fruity and in the fourth part add mix fruit essence, green food colour and red tutty fruit and mix well.

First take rose ball and make it flat and add vanilla both and cover it properly. Then take pineapple ball and flatten and add this ball and cover it and lastly take mix fruit gola and cover it properly and give a cylindrical shape.

Then put in refrigerator for an hour and then cut into pieces and you can see cassatta sandesh is ready to serve.

ALMOND COCOA ROLLS

Ingredients :
- Roasted almond powder ½ cup
- Grated khoya – ½ cup
- Cocoa powder – 1 ½ tsp
- Cardamom powder – 1 tsp
- Vanilla essence – 1 tsp
- Powder sugar – ½ cup
- Milk – ½ cup
- Clarified butter – 1 tsp
- Dry coconut powder – ¾ cup

Let's Cook :

Take a deep pan. Boil sugar, milk and clarified butter till sugar melts and it is lightly thickened. Add grated khoya, almond powder, coconut powder, cocoa powder and cook till fat releases and it forms into a loose dough. Add vanilla essence and cardamom powder and mix well allow it to cool.

Roll into small balls and sprinkles almond flakes and serve.

SWEET PEANUTS

Ingredients :

- 500 g peanuts
- 50 g cornflour
- 150 g granulated sugar
- 100 ml warm water

Let's Cook :

Heat the peanuts in a pan. Dry fry them until very crisp set aside.

Heat the sugar and 100 ml warm water in a pan, stirring until the sugar dissolves continue to stir until the thin syrup bubble, stir in the peanuts. Gradually add the cornflour until the peanuts are well coated with the syrup. Remove, let cool slightly and serve.

LEMONGRASS ICE-CREAM

Ingredients :

- Fresh cream – 200 ml
- Full fat milk – 500 ml
- Chopped lemon grass – ½ cup
- Cornflour – 1 ½ tbsp
- Sugar – 3 tbsp
- Fennel seeds powder – 1 tsp
- Water – 2-3 tbsp
- Lemon leaves – 10-12
- Lemon zest – 1 tsp
- Green food colour few drops

Let's Cook :

In a blender jar take lemon grass, lemon leaves and water and grind it to a smooth paste and strain and keep aside.

In a deep sauce pan take milk, cornflour and sugar and stir so that no lumps are formed. Boil till it thickens stirring continuously. Allow it to cool add 200 ml fresh cream, lemon grass paste, fennel seeds, lemon zest, food colour and mix well. Pour in air tight container and set in freezer for at least 5-6 hrs. Then remove from freezer and beat until smooth and again freeze until properly set serve the ice-cream garnished with lemon leaves and lemon zest.

GLOSSARY OF INGREDIENTS

- Garam masala – All spice powder
- Hing – Asafoetida
- Tej patta – Bay leaves
- Elaichi – green cardamom
- Ajwain – Carom seeds
- Dalchini – Cinnamon
- Laung – Cloves
- Dhaniya - Coriander (Cilantro)
- Jeera – Cumin
- Amchoor – Dried mango
- Kalonji – Onion seeds
- Methi – Fenugreek
- Adrak – Cunger
- Lahsun – Garlic
- Gur – Jaggery
- Kali mirch – Black Pepper
- Anardana – Pomegranate seeds
- Khus-Khus – Poppy seeds
- Gulabjal – Rose water
- Kala namak – Rock salt
- Til – Sesame
- Haldi – Turmeric
- Pudina – Mint
- Saunf – Fennel seeds
- Jaiphal – Nutmeg
- Sarson - Mustard

KNOW YOUR MEASUREMENTS

Vegetables

Carrots	1 Cup	100 g
Cabbage (Shred)	1 Cup	60 g
French beans (sliced)	1 Cup	80 g
Baby corn	8 no's	100 g
Spinach after cleaning	1 bunch	110 g
Tomatoes	3 or 4 medium	450 g
Bell peppers diced medium	1 cup	
Asparagus fresh	16 to 20 spears	450 g
Onions chopped	2 ½ cups 3 large	450 g
Zucchini sliced	4 – 4 cups	
Water chest nuts canned	1 cup	225 g

Cereals

Wheat flour	1 Cup	100 g
Jawar flour	1 Cup	90 g
Ragi	1 Cup	90 g
Maize flour	1 Cup	80 g
Bajra flour	1 Cup	80 g
All purpose flour	1 Cup	80 g
Broken wheat	1 Cup	120 g
Semolina (Suji)	1 Cup	200 g
Rice	1 Cup	200 g

Fruits

Apples diced	2 ¾ cups -3 medium	450 g
Bananas	3-4 medium	450 g
Dates pitted	2 ½ cups	450 g
Pears fresh & sliced	2 cups	450 g
Strawberrys	1 ¾ cups sliced	450 g
Grapes seedless	2 ½ cups	450 g
Pineapple canned slices	10 slices	590 ml
Cherries canned	2 cups	450 g

Nuts

Almond silvered	1 cup	150 g
Pistachios unshelled	½ cup	115 g
Walnuts chopped	½ cup	55 g
Pecans chopped	½ cup	55 g

Miscellaneous

Noodles	1 cup	100 g
Puffed rice	1 cup	20 g
Peanut butter	2 cups	510 g
Honey	1 1/3 cups	450 g
Chocolate chips	1 cup	170 g
Icing sugar	3 ¾ cups	450 g
Brown sugar	2 ¼ cups	450 g
Coconut shredded	2 2/3 cups	200 g
Whipping cream frozen	3 cups	225 g

Conversions

1 Cup	200 ml
1/2 Cup	100 ml
1/3 Cup	80 ml
3/4 Cup	150 ml

1 ½ Cup	300 ml
1 Soup bowl	1 ½ Cups
1 sp	5 ml
1 glass	200 ml
1 kg	22 pounds

Printed in the United States
By Bookmasters